LETTERS TO HER

From the Diary of Aaditya Bajpai

Copyright

A Note To The Readers

Dear Reader,

Welcome to *Letters to Her*, a journey that is as much yours as it is mine. These pages hold fragments of thoughts, whispered longings, and truths wrapped in the language of poetry. But who is "Her"? Is she the muse? A memory? A dream? Or perhaps "Her" is a reflection of your own hidden desires, fears, and hopes.

This book is not meant to give you answers rather it is here to pose questions, to stir echoes in your heart, and to guide you to places within yourself you may have forgotten to explore. The letters are intimate, yet universal; deeply personal, yet they resonate with anyone who has loved, lost, or dared to hope.

Here's where the challenge begins. At the end of this book, you'll find a blank page. It's not just a page—it's a mirror, a canvas, a doorway. I invite you to pick up your pen and write a letter to your own "Her." Who is she to you? Is she a person, an idea, or a feeling? Let the ink unravel your truth. Write her a letter as raw, as vulnerable, and as honest as you dare.

Will you accept this challenge? Will you let your soul speak?

The page awaits.

With love,
Aaditya.

About The Author

I, *Aaditya Bajpai*, born in 2002 in Uttar Pradesh, am an Author, Poet, and Singer. I have been practicing music since class 3, and today my original songs are available on all major music streaming platforms. Writing poems has been a long-time passion of mine, though I kept them private for many years. Since the start of 2020, I have been sharing my poetry on my Instagram handle, gaining appreciation from a growing audience.

I have contributed as a Co-Author to many anthologies, and my first book as a solo author, *The Unadvised Writings*, brought me immense happiness following its release. Now, I invite you all on another intimate journey with *Letters to Her*, and I hope you all enjoy reading it more than how much I enjoyed writing it.

You can follow me on Instagram :

@_aadiwrites and also *@_aadimusic*

Follow me on Spotify

@Aaditya Bajpai

An Ode to Romanticism: A Reverie of Love through Ethereal Metaphors of Sky, Cloud, Flowers, and Air

"tumhare siwa aur koi pasand hi nahi aata aaj kal"

Coming out of the spiritual and traditional holds of the conventional genres of poetry, the late 18th and 19th centuries provided for a poetic movement that was dedicated whole-heartedly towards the interior worlds of feeling, in opposition to the mannered formalism and disciplined scientific enquiry of the enlightenment era that preceded it. This movement is what is termed as Romanticism. Poets like Mary Shelley, Mary Robinson, Charlotte Turner Smith, William Wordsworth, Samuel Taylor Coleridge, John Keats, Percy Shelley, William Blake, Lord Byron, and so on, are huge examples of this ideology of literature, and produced works that expressed spontaneous feelings, found parallels to their emotional lives in the natural world, and celebrated creativity rather than logic.

The spirit of Romanticism wasn't just to counter the ideology upheld by the Enlightenment era, rather it was majorly dedicated to celebrating the creativity of life and emotions by the use of metaphors and paralleling the natural world with human emotions, and love being the epitome of the same. Nature is a substantial presence in Romantic poetry, functioning as a teacher and companion. The poets viewed their art as mediation between humanity and nature and would set their human dramas on her stage. The Romantic wanderer and vicariously the reader would learn his or her place in the universe by journeying through nature's dark spaces and exotic dream lands. The mysterious, monstrous, and strange are all Romantic era poetic predilections.

This romantic era emphasised intuition and imagination over reason, everyday language over inscrutable poetic form, and the pastoral over the urban. Imagination is the gateway to transcendence, and the poet filters powerful emotions and emotive responses, translating them into an accessible poet form. The arguably extreme idealism of Romanticism was characterised by a search for immortality, imperfections and pure love, in parlance with everyday life.

The Sky: Muse for Poets

"chaand ko dekhu, ya tumhe
Baat toh ek hi hai na."

The sky has been an eternal muse for poets and artists alike, its endless expanse serving as a captivating metaphor for the depth and breadth of love. The sky's vastness evokes a sense of infinity, mirroring the boundless nature of the love that we feel for another. The clouds that dance across the sky are akin to the ebbs and flows of a relationship, representing moments of turbulence as well as serenity. The sunrise and sunset, in all their resplendence, capture the start and end of a love story, embodying the promise of new beginnings and the acceptance of closure. The stars that shimmer in the night sky, like diamonds in the firmament, symbolise the fleeting yet profound moments of happiness shared with our beloved. The moon, in all its mystique and enchantment, encapsulates the magic and transformative power of love, illuminating our path to finding meaning and purpose. Ultimately, the sky reminds us of the universality of love, a force that binds us together and gives our lives greater meaning.

Indeed, the sky continues to inspire and captivate us, with its ever-changing hues and moods. The shifting shades of blue and pink during dawn and dusk reflect the nuances of love, its shades and intensities. The wispy clouds that adorn the sky, taking on a myriad of shapes and forms, are reminiscent of the playful and whimsical nature of love. The thundering clouds and lightning bolts that occasionally pierce the sky are akin to the challenges and obstacles that we must navigate in a relationship. And yet, just as the sky eventually clears after a storm, so too can love endure and thrive despite the challenges that may arise.

Moreover, the sky's beauty and majesty serve as a reminder of the power of love to transcend our individual selves and connect us to something greater than ourselves. The vastness of the sky reminds us that our love is but a small yet significant part of the grand tapestry of life, a testament to the beauty and wonder of the universe. Whether it is the quiet stillness of a starry night or the vibrant hues of a sunset, the sky is a canvas that reflects the myriad emotions and experiences that love brings into our lives. It is a reminder that love is not just a feeling, but a journey that takes us to new horizons, enriching our lives and elevating our souls.

Aaditya Bajpai

Flowers: Reminder That Love Is Eternal

Flowers have long been revered as one of nature's most exquisite creations, a symbol of love and beauty that transcends cultures and time. Each petal, delicate and intricate, is a testament to the wonder and complexity of life. The vibrant colors that adorn flowers, ranging from soft pastels to bold hues, evoke a sense of vitality and passion that is reminiscent of the intensity of love.

Like love, flowers have the power to transform us, to uplift our spirits and bring joy to our hearts. Their sweet fragrance and gentle sway in the breeze evoke a sense of calm and serenity, reminding us to appreciate the simple pleasures of life. The different varieties of flowers, each with its own unique beauty and symbolism, offer a rich tapestry of emotions and experiences that are akin to the nuances of love.

From the dainty and fragile beauty of a rose to the robust and hearty sunflower, flowers represent the diversity and complexity of love. The intricacy of a lily, with its soft petals and complex patterns, captures the depth and richness of love's many layers. The velvety texture of a carnation, with its vibrant colours and sweet scent, embodies the sensual and passionate nature of love.

In essence, flowers are a metaphor for love, a reminder that beauty and love are inseparable. They remind us that even in the darkest moments, there is always beauty to be found, a ray of hope that can light up our lives. They remind us that love is not just an emotion, but a force that can inspire us to be our best selves, to see the world in a new and beautiful way. Whether it is a single bloom or a fragrant bouquet, flowers remind us of the power and magic of love, a force that can transform our lives and touch our souls.

Air: Metaphor of Love

The air that surrounds us, invisible yet all-pervading, is a poetic and ethereal metaphor for love. Just as the air is essential to sustain life, so too is love necessary to nourish the soul. The gentle breeze that caresses our skin, cool and refreshing, represents the comfort and warmth that love brings to our hearts.

The air can also be unpredictable and tempestuous, like the ups and downs of a relationship. The winds that gust and swirl, tugging at our hair and clothes, mirror the turbulence and challenges that love can bring. But just as the air eventually calms and settles, so too can love endure and thrive despite the difficulties.

Moreover, the air is a reminder of the intangible yet powerful nature of love. Just as we cannot see or touch the air, so too is love a force that transcends the physical realm. It is a feeling that fills our hearts and souls, giving us the strength and courage to face the world. The air is also a symbol of freedom and liberation, a reminder that love is not meant to be possessive or suffocating. Like the air that allows birds to soar and clouds to drift, love should give us the space and freedom to grow and evolve as individuals.

In essence, the air is a beautiful and evocative metaphor for love, reminding us of the delicate yet enduring nature of this powerful emotion. Whether it is the gentle breeze that cools our skin or the gusting winds that challenge us, the air reminds us that love is a force that can bring us to greater heights and give us courage to embrace life to the fullest.

Clouds: The Ebb and Flow of Love

The clouds that drift lazily across the sky are a poetic and enchanting metaphor for love, evoking a sense of wonder and mystery. Like love, clouds come in a multitude of forms and shapes, each one unique and breath-taking in its own way. The delicate wisps of a cirrus cloud, high and wispy, embody the ethereal and intangible nature of love, while the dramatic and imposing form of a cumulonimbus cloud reflects the power and intensity of this complex emotion.

Clouds also have the ability to transform and shape the world around us, much like the way love can alter and shape our lives. The gentle puffs of a cumulus cloud can cast dappled shadows on the ground, creating a sense of enchantment and magic that is reminiscent of the joy and wonder that love can bring. The looming form of a thundercloud, with its dark and ominous presence, is a stark reminder of the challenges and obstacles that love can pose.

Furthermore, the movement of clouds across the sky serves as a metaphor for the ebb and flow of love. Just as clouds drift and move across the sky, so too can love evolve and change over time. The shifting hues of a sunset or the vivid colours of a sunrise, reflected on the clouds, remind us of the endless possibilities and beauty that love can bring.

In essence, clouds are a beautiful and evocative metaphor for love, capturing the complexity and wonder of this powerful emotion. Whether it is the delicate and ethereal wisps of a cirrus cloud or the imposing and dramatic form of a cumulonimbus cloud, the clouds remind us that love is a force that can shape and transform our lives, leaving an indelible mark on our hearts and souls.

Romanticism

Romanticism is the heartbeat of the soul, the melody that stirs our hearts and fills us with a sense of wonder and awe. It is the brushstroke that paints our world with beauty and colour, the spark that ignites our passion, and the fire that drives our dreams. Through romanticism, we connect with the world around us on a deeper level, embracing the complexities and nuances of life with a sense of reverence and awe. It is the force that moves us, the inspiration that drives us forward, and the foundation upon which our most cherished memories are built.

Romanticism infuses our days with meaning and purpose, reminding us of the beauty and majesty that surrounds us at every turn. It is the laughter that bubbles up from within us, the tears that we shed, and the joy that fills our hearts. It is the promise of a new beginning, the hope that fuels our dreams, and the faith that sustains us through the darkest of times.

In essence, romanticism is the soul of our existence, the essence of our being that connects us to the world around us. It is the light that illuminates our path, the magic that makes our hearts sing, and the wonder that fills our days with joy and delight. Without romanticism, life would be a mere existence, a hollow shell of what it could be. But with romanticism, we soar to greater heights, embracing the wonder and beauty of life in all its splendour.

Aaditya Bajpai

The Letters

Aaditya Bajpai

Walking Down

Walking down the shallows,
I found myself lost,
in the sunset.

The aging sun,
glared dimly at me.
There, with her, I met.

Her eyes were shining,
and the world seemed to be in it.
With each moment passing by,
I felt like I was going down in debt.

She held my hand,
though a stranger.
A wave passed through my veins,
washing down all my regret.

My pain,
it was gone.
The shallowness,
it was gone.
There was a new light,
we made a vow,
that in moments of love and sorrow,
we will give each other, hope.

Through the lights

Through the lights I see,
You playing with your hair,
Smiling so endearingly,
That at that particular jiff,
The evening becomes the most dazzling
it has ever been.
The blink of your eyes,
sends fair speechless messages.
The texts of those messages,
are something that only in my dreams I have seen.
As the night grows darker,
all I pray for is to make this an everlasting night.
Or to stop the time at that particular moment, when you smile.
Through the lights I see,
Even the word fair , in front of you,
is not so fair.

Cookie, Coffee & You

Coffee is all that you think about.
You, every sip, every moment of warmth,
consumed by the grind of your own thoughts.
But I? I am consumed by you, the way you hold that cup,
as if it were an anchor to everything I have yet to say.
Hopelessness is all that the cookie thinks about— crumbled and forgotten,
waiting to be dipped, yearning for someone to notice its fragility.
How does that work? I don't know.
But somehow, it mirrors my own longing
for you to reach across and just— touch.
You sit, sipping your coffee, and I watch,
my tea blossoming in the wind of your love,
as though your gaze could be the sun to my fragile petals.
I try to pull away, but my eyes are tethered to you,
like gravity, and you, an orbit I can't leave.
The cookie waits— hopeless, desperate,
for your hand to break it,
and yet I am the one broken,
watching, waiting for you to see me
the way you see your coffee.
The vanilla cake, that thing you love and I loathe
suddenly carries the scent of everything I need.
It isn't just vanilla anymore, but your essence,
your laughter, your quiet grace, taking over the bakery,
making everything better because you exist in it.
I could never leave this space,
this bakery, as long as your presence sweetens the air,

and every glance from you turns every taste

into something I never knew I craved.

Aaditya Bajpai

You

You know why
I always look at you
and smile ?

You know why
I always say to you
that with you I am alive ?

You know why
I glow, when
you lay your hand on me ?

They say,
the moon is nothing
without its moonlight.
The stars,
they complete the night.

And you,
you are my moonlight.
You are my star.
When darkness surrounds me,
you come and give me light, and
take away all of my plight.

Sky

In the shadows
of the sky,
I see you.

The bird, singing,
echoing, in the hushed blues.
I wave my hand,
the starless stranger, waves back.

Winds of the autumn, gushing,
touching the old, falling leaves.
Taking away, the colour, and
taking away its life.

Nevertheless, I wander
in pursuit of happiness
in a hurry, for the haze
arrives in no time.

I found you, while seeking
the truth, of life.
Sunshine, isn't far enough,
for I possess the will,
to see it.

The pursuit of happiness,
is you, for you're the answer,
I have been, so long,
wandering for.
In the shadows, of the sky,
I see you.

Aaditya Bajpai

Within You I Find

I dissolve in you,
your body, and your soul
dwelling into me.
Staying awake amidst,
the *shorgul* of town.
Your smell, your essence
is enough to put life
into the dreary desert of my heart.
Meeting you every now and then,
it all doesn't feel enough.
For like every heart requires,
the stream of blood to flow through it.
I require, you to engulf within me,
and our souls, they merge,
so intensely, that even the
cupid would fall onto earth,
to seek our blessings.
I want to die in you,
you still keep me alive.
I want to lose thyself in your darkness,
thee still drag me out to light.
I don't deserve you,
you still embrace every
nickle of blood, that flows in me.
This isn't a filthy manifestation
nor it is my search to survive.
This is love, the love,
within you I strive,
within you I find.

Yellow Days

Do I begin with your forehead,
pressing a kiss like a promise?
Or do you start,
your lips finding mine
before I can gift you the yellow flowers
and the yellow hairband?
No— the better thing
is slipping the band into your hair,
then tucking the flowers behind your ear,
deliberate, careful,
as though arranging sunlight.
We lace up our canvas shoes—
mine black, yours yellow,
the soft rhythm of our steps
carrying us toward a flower market.
You pick a single yellow bloom,
delicate in your hands, and place it over my ear.
You laugh, tell me I look cute that way,
and I believe you,
because your laughter
is the only truth I trust.
Later,
we'll argue about Wes Anderson—
you'll insist on *Asteroid City,*
and I'll champion *The Grand Budapest Hotel.*
But somehow,
we'll end up with *Fantastic Mr. Fox,*
your hand on mine,
our story unravelling
in the space between frames.
Every moment,
wrapped in yellow.

Aaditya Bajpai

Vanilla Cake

You are the vanilla cake,
light and soft like a whispered secret,
the kind that fills the room with warmth
without ever raising its voice.
Your sweetness is quiet,
unspoken but known—
the fragrance of vanilla clings to the air
like the memory of a touch that never fades.
Each layer of you is simple,
but underneath,
there's something rich,
like a hidden garden blooming just for me.
When I cut into you,
I find not just flavour,
but the very essence of comfort,
a softness that crumbles in my hands,
yet holds together in the sweetest way.
Your frosting is the delicate promise,
the gentle edge that makes me believe
everything that's good and pure
could exist in a single bite.
And though the world spins outside,
I'll always choose you,
the quiet beauty,
the warmth,
the perfect simplicity,
waiting to be savoured.

Dishes

I'll cook for you like I'm a pancake
flipping in all the wrong directions,
but somehow landing just right.
The kitchen will smell like chaos,
a mix of garlic and forgotten thoughts,
and I'll stir the pot like I'm trying to
find the right words that never seem to come.
The onions will cry, but I'll pretend
I'm not the one making them sob.
I'll boil pasta like I'm waiting for a text
that's not coming, but I don't mind—
I'll drown my impatience in sauce.
The tomatoes will soften,
just like how my heart does when you smile.
When the meal is ready,
I'll serve it with a spoon as a microphone,
talking to the plates like they're old friends
who've been waiting for this moment.
You'll laugh at how the salad is a bit too much
and the bread a bit too burnt,
but I'll pretend it's perfect,
because to me, it always will be.
Then, when the food is eaten
and the dishes need washing,
I'll scrub them like I'm trying to remove
the world's weight from my shoulders.
I'll make the glasses shine like stars,
and the silverware will glint like
little pieces of stolen sunlight.
And when I'm done,
I'll wipe the counters and pretend
I'm wiping away all the worries I have,
but really, I'm just hoping you notice
how much I care.

Aaditya Bajpai

The Idea of You

Because for me,
even the idea of you
is a comfort I cannot explain.
It is the warmth of a promise,
a shadow that holds my hand
even though I am alone.
I have wandered through faces,
through fleeting moments of connection,
but none of them fill the space
where you once stood,
or where I still imagine you,
half-drawn in the corners of my mind,
a ghost of possibility.
You are the picture I never paint,
the song I never finish,
the dream I never wake from.
In your absence,
I build you from fragments—
a smile, a gesture,
the way your laughter feels like home.
I have tasted the reality of someone else,
tried to make it enough,
but it is hollow,
a mask too thin to wear.
They are not you.
They never will be.
And so,
I return to the idea of you,
that soft, untouchable version
that never disappoints,
never changes.
In my mind, you are perfect,
a reflection of what could be,

Aaditya Bajpai

and I am content to keep you there—
unbroken, unbothered by the weight of flesh.
Because for me,
even the idea of you
is better than the reality of someone else.
It is enough,
and yet,
it is everything I will never have.

Aaditya Bajpai

A Story of a Ghost Who Falls in Love

I exist in half-light,
between the pulse of the living
and the silence of the dead.
I am the ghost alive—
a whisper in the crowded room,
a shadow trailing footstep that does not stop for me.

I fell in love one evening,
when the world was tinted amber,
and you stood at the edge of the park,
your laughter cutting through the air
like the first notes of a forgotten song.
You didn't see me then,
but I saw you.

I saw the way you tilted your head to listen,
as though the breeze carried secrets.
I wanted to be that breeze,
to brush past your skin,
to whisper my name into
the hollow of your ear.

You walked home that night,
and I followed,
silent as I always am,
but louder in your presence.
Each step brought me closer
to the realization
that I was haunting not the world,
but myself.

Days passed,
and I lingered.
I lingered in the spaces you forgot to fill,

Aaditya Bajpai

in the book you left open on your table,
in the tea you drank halfway before losing interest.
I watched as you lived,
a life full of things I could never touch,
yet I was there—alive in my longing,
dead in my inability to belong.
One night, you looked up,
your eyes searching the empty air
as though you felt me.

"Who's there?" you asked,
and for the first time,
I wanted to answer.
But ghosts do not speak.
Instead, I reached out,
letting my presence settle
in the cold brush of wind against your cheek.
You shivered,
and I wanted to say,
"It's me. I'm here.

I've been here, alive and ghost,
waiting for you to notice."
I am the ghost who fell in love—

alive in the ache of wanting,

dead in the impossibility of having.

And still, I haunt you,

not to scare,

but to be seen,

to leave some trace of myself

in the space you inhabit.

Aaditya Bajpai

Between Holding & Letting Go

There is a place between grasping and release,
a trembling space where I find you.
You are the breath I cannot exhale,
the weight in my hand that refuses to settle
but slips through my fingers
like water pretending to be stone.
I can't hold you,
not the way I want to—
not without breaking the fragile edges
of what we are.
Love isn't something to be clenched;
it bruises in captivity,
wilts under the heat of too much want.
But letting go?
That feels like erasing a part of myself,
like asking the ocean to forget its waves,
or the earth to give up its gravity.
You are woven into me,
a thread so fine I could never pull it free
without unravelling entirely.
And so,
I stand here,
on the threshold of staying and leaving,
holding your name like a prayer
that neither reaches heaven nor falls silent.
Perhaps love is this—
not the possession of another soul,
but the willingness
to carry their absence
and still call it beautiful.

In The Shadow of David

I see you,
like Michelangelo saw David—
not as stone,
but as something waiting to emerge,
every curve and flaw
already perfect before the chisel touched marble.

You stand,
a quiet masterpiece,
the weight of the world balanced
in the line of your jaw,
your gaze holding something
that feels eternal,
even in its softness.

Do I trace the marble of your shoulders
with my fingertips,
or do I step back,
awed by the shape you take
even when untouched?

We are like that statue,
unfinished in places only we can see,
chipped edges and smoothed lines
telling stories of hands
that dared to reach too far.

And still—
still,
I cannot look away.
Perhaps,
I am the sculptor
and you are the stone.

Or perhaps,
you are David,
and I am the light
pouring through the gallery,
trying desperately
to frame you just right.

Eventually,
like the statue,
you will outlast everything.
And if I cannot stand beside you,
I will stand in your shadow—
forever shaped by the art of loving you.

Eventually

Eventually,
the paths we walk will fold into one,
like rivers forgetting their names
as they spill into the sea.
Even if you are not there,
I will carry the echo of your footsteps,
the imprint of your smile,
a map traced in whispers and glances.

Eventually,
the silence between us
will grow into a song,
its melody shaped by the moments
we almost touched,
the words we left unsaid.
I will hum it to myself
on nights when stars feel closer than you.

Eventually,
I will find you in the spaces
you never meant to leave—
the crease in a paperback,
the chipped edge of a coffee mug.
You'll be there
in the way the light bends
through rain-soaked windows,
in the way the wind
shifts through autumn leaves.
Even if you are gone,
I will still reach for you—
through distance,
through time,
through all the ways the world

Aaditya Bajpai

tries to keep us apart.

Eventually,
I will belong to you
like the tide belongs to the moon,
inevitable, unbroken,
a pull too quiet to name
but always there.

Aaditya Bajpai

Spilled Water and Chopsticks

The glow of neon catches your skin—
pink and purple painting shadows on the curve of your cheek.
We are haloed in "good vibes only,"
but the way you look at me is the only gospel I believe.
You wrestle with chopsticks,
a clumsy dance of wood and slick noodles.
Every spicy mouthful steals a blink,
your lashes flutter twice like a nervous spell—
and I am enchanted.
My food cools, untouched.
Yours vanishes, each bite disappearing
into the story of your hunger.
When I offer you more,
you laugh,
slide your plate too far,
topple the glass of water
between us.
"Why didn't I drink this?" you mutter,
grabbing napkins like they're answers.
I want to ask if you are always this messy
with things you care for.
But I only watch
as you swipe at the spill,
as though it's urgent.
When it's cleaned,
I pull my plate between us,
a quiet offering,
a bridge.
You lean forward,
foreheads grazing—
a fragile hello.
"Don't move," you whisper,
your breath pooling in the air between us.

Aaditya Bajpai

"Stay like this. Close. Like elephants. Did you know they do this?
Heads together, a greeting."
I don't tell you

I already knew.

I don't tell you

I want every moment with you to feel like this—

strange, and full, and alive.

Her

Whenever I look at a sunflower
it'd remind me of you.
Sunflowers are metaphors for
the people around whom you feel alive.
I have an open field inside of me
wherein the wind echoes your laugh.
The open field has always been filled
with roses, that your presence has watered.
If this is what the poets call love, then I've
laced far too many notebooks with the idea of you.

How everything eventually is about you?
How sometimes i go sleepless at nights, but then
How I yearn to sleep a little bit more
because you came into my dreams.
How I grieve when I am not close to you?
But then what is grief, if not love persevering.
What is grief, if not love with no place to go,
that corners in your eyes, and
in the hollow part of your chest?

What is love, if not the poem
scratched on the walls of my throat.
How I'd want to linger near the door
uncomfortably, rather than leaving.
How I'd want you to forget your scarf
and come back later, to find it.
What is love, if not everything that I feel for you?
For it was when you allowed me to enter
your world, when I was scared of mine.

I want to peel oranges with you,
on a wintered evening in Tokyo.
I want to have walk with you
I'll hold your hands and you can hold mine.

I kiss you on your forehead,

Aaditya Bajpai

you kiss me on my lips.
I'll take you to this coffee shop, I know of
you can get your favourite latte and I'll get that too.
You'll drink it hot, and then burn your tongue
and suddenly start complaining that I didn't warn.

Then I'll take my handkerchief out and smile, before
I wipe that bit of cream that's there on your lips.
Then I kiss you on your forehead again, only
you'd not expect it this time.

It is my love for you that I envy the winds
for I wish I were the wind, so I could touch you
softly on your skin, whisper sweet things in your ear, and give you
the blanket of my love.

Someday when then scenery becomes a memory,
what would I want to remember?
I want to remember you, from now on, always and forever.
A hundred years from now,
and you'd still find me engaged
in the subtle art of loving you.
I'll be writing poetry, and it'll be about you every day.
For what good is poetry if it's not about you?

Aaditya Bajpai

When Will I Get to Love You?

Maybe I am compromised way too much
to sit still and watch all these lovers love.
How they all sit together, hold hands,
look into each other's eyes, smiling, and
blooming at the mildest of touches.
It is all so beautiful, looking at which
even the cupid falls on earth as such.

I remember this quote from Rumi, i.e.,
"I love you from my soul,
because if ever my heart stops and I die,
I'll still keep on loving you".

Looking at all these lovers makes me
want to crave my own, which is you.
To hold your hands, will it all be true?
When will I finally meet you?
So, I don't have to sit and watch
all these lovers love, all alone
without you.

Aaditya Bajpai

The Poem Is You

In that moment I saw you wandering the streets
enjoying life so endearingly, and I fell in love.
The feeling was unknown, yet it had a friendly odour.
Something which you have never known,
still, you want to befriend it, nevertheless.

It is my love for you that I envy the winds
for I wish I were the wind, so I could touch you
softly on your skin, whisper sweet things in your ear,
and give you the blanket of my love.

This world is such a chaotic place.
A sphere of unexpressed emotions and emoted sentiments.
And I pity the ones who's don't get to see
what all love can bring to you. Like it did to me.

The power of love is astonishing.
I have seen people heal just because they were in love.
It's surprising how far can a human heart go
to protect itself and the ones it loves.
And my love is You. I can feel you everywhere,
for you have taken over every corner of my heart.

It was when I met you,
I didn't feel so lost or aimless.
Because even if there was nothing else for me,
it felt like loving you was what I was made for,
and it didn't matter what anyone thought of me,
and it didn't matter if I didn't have any other big plans for myself,
as long as I got to love you.

Someday when then scenery becomes a memory,
what would I want to remember?
I want to remember you, from now on, always and forever.
A hundred years from now, and
you'd still find me engaged in the subtle art of loving you.
I'll be writing poetry, and it'll be about you every day.

Aaditya Bajpai

For what good is poetry if it's not about you?

I've a lot of feeling for you. You're kind.
We'll kiss, grow old, walk around.
Light months will fly over us
Like snowy stars.

Aaditya Bajpai

Asylum

Whenever I look at a sunflower
it'd remind me of you.
Sunflowers are metaphors for
the people around whom you feel alive.
I have an open field inside of me
wherein the wind echoes your laugh.
The open field has always been filled
with roses, that your presence has watered.
If this is what the poets call love, then I've
laced far too many notebooks with the idea of you.
How everything eventually is about you?
How sometimes i go sleepless at nights, but then
How I yearn to sleep a little bit more
because you came into my dreams.
How I grieve when I am not close to you?
But then what is grief, if not love persevering.
What is grief, if not love with no place to go,
that corners in your eyes, and
in the hollow part of your chest?
What is love, if not the poem
scratched on the walls of my throat.
How I'd want to linger near the door
uncomfortably, rather than leaving.
How I'd want you to forget your scarf
and come back later, to find it.
What is love, if not everything that I feel for you?
For it was when you allowed me to enter
your world, when I was scared of mine.
Toh aakhir Kaha chala hai man ka rasta?
Tumhare paas.

The Art of Letting Go

Loving someone dearly is what we do the best.
Probably better than breathing, we love.
We cling close to it, aware that
we in no way can control it.
Everything seems to be wonderful,
Filled with colours, rainbows and lights.
We want to stay close, and keep them close.
We want to hold them, and take them home.
Touching of toes, meeting of lips,
Making love with your every bit.
Beginning the days with their name
And wanting to end the same with their breath.
Adamant and ignorant of the fact that,
All of it is just holding roses,
until the thorns press against your fingers.
Letting go is an art of necessity.
We do not want it, but we have to master it.
It wasn't until I saw in her eyes, that
irrespective of what I feel, it will never be the same for her.
Even Stephen King once said, that sometimes in life
You have to just let the bird go, for
You know it's not meant to be caged.
When those thorns press so hard,
That you realise that it's time to let go,
For it just means that we are all humans
Incapable of holding on to everything,
especially when it hurts the most.
The only barrier to letting go is hope,
We hope that maybe something somehow will work out,
But it never does. It's always the thorns over the roses.
So, in the end, the whole of loving someone,
Becomes an act of letting go.
So, take you moment, and take you time,
And bid that farewell with all your heart.

December 22nd

It's the 22nd of December, 6:05 pm,
exactly two months since I last wrote to you.
Have you ever yearned for something
that wasn't even yours to begin with?
Because I know I have been lost, since so
long, in something, in you?
The leaves of autumn have fallen dead, and
here I am wanting to have an orange with you.
This winter, it tells me, to finally stand up to you
and tell you that I am so much in love with you.
It's like even the ghost in my closet,
is screaming to let it all out.

But it's you we are talking about,
in front whom I am nothing but an idle candle,
burning in its own flame, and
standing still nevertheless.
My heart skips a beat and my world stops
as my gaze takes in the sight of her stunning form,
clad in her *kurti* and a *dupatta*.
My eyes flicker my heart flutters,
as I gaze upon the goddess of perfection.

But it's December, the month of letting go.
December holds so much,
the end of best times, and
closure for all that was lost.
A month so hopeful, yet
carries heaviness in its frost.
Maybe this time, I'll say it all too.
On Christmas' eve, I'll meet you at the golden hour, standing
hopefully, you'll be in my sight,
and, I'll give you the yellow flower.

Then? I'll leave it to December
to teach me that, new beginnings,
don't really require new calendars.

Because I know, it's always you.
I'll spend my eternity, in
perfecting the subtle art of loving you.
Today, tomorrow and the day after,
every bit of my love, will be about you.

Aaditya Bajpai

I Waited, You Didn't Come

The leaves have started turning to
shades of yellow, orange and red.
October has finally arrived.
They say that the turning of colours
Is to protect the leaves from cold temperatures.
It's October 6 today, and I am writing this to you.
The evening today is nice and warm,
Though it's about to turn cold.
I came nearby the lake we used to visit,
Walked a bit, and even left a note
for you to read, between the pages of your notebook.
The note said, "meet me by the lakeside, we will sit and talk".
The lake was still today, and had turned
Orange, as if the sun was drowning in it.
The sky was still alive, while I waited for you.
I asked myself today,
Did you ever want to go far away?
Where would you go?
But I couldn't find an answer,
So, I waited for you to give me one.
"Aaj walk Karne chalen? Shaam ko, beside the lake?", the note said.
It was getting dark, as 2 hours had passed.
I still wanted the answer, and I wanted you there.
I kept walking and talking to the sun.
It didn't last long, as the sun finally rested in the lake.
It was getting dark, and I kept waiting.
Maybe the note was misplaced,
The wind was strong today.
And a lot many reasons I gave myself
to hold myself from crying.
"I will wait some other day", I said to myself.
What happened today?
I waited; you didn't come.

The Moon is Pretty, Isn't It?

I have been romanticising a lot of things ever since I have met you,
because honestly, I never thought I'd find
what I have always been looking for, that
the one in my life would be so near.
I started off with wanting to peel oranges with you,
on a wintered evening in Tokyo?
With us in that blanket, you got for me
with Spiderman printed on it! I just
I just want to take you by the hand, because
it's you, it's always been you to understand.
Now I say let's take a walk together, on that
same wintered evening in Tokyo! I can,
I can hold your hands and you can hold mine.
I can kiss you on your forehead, you can kiss me
on my lips. Then again, we continue our walk.

I'll take you to this coffee shop, I know of
you can get your favourite latte and I'll get that too.
You'll drink it hot, and then burn your tongue
and suddenly start complaining that I didn't warn.
Then I'll take my handkerchief out and smile, before
I wipe that bit of cream that's there on your lips.
Then I kiss you on your forehead again, only
you'd not expect it this time.
We'll see each other through our eyes,
and eventually we'll kiss, just like that.
We can then go on walking again, this time
to that beach you like. Walking barefoot.

You'll tell me,
"See the moon looks so pretty, isnt it?"
And I'll just keep staring at you and say,
"indeed it is Beautiful".
Hearing my voice you'd suddenly
look at me, and I'll instantly look at the moon.
You'll know, I called you my moon, but
you won't say. There will be a blush on your face

Aaditya Bajpai

and then I'll eventually look at you again because
that's all that I want to see in that wintered evening in Tokyo.

I'll then look at you and keep looking at you
because even God's grace couldn't be
as beautiful as that sight of yours.
And then I'll say, I love you. I'll say,
*"Even a hundred years from now, and I'll still
be engaged in the subtle art of loving you"*.
I'll then walk you home and you'll say once again
"The moon did look pretty today, right?"
and I'll again look at your eyes and say,
"It always does".

Aaditya Bajpai

Muse

Lucky are those who inspire artists,
who become the stroke of a brush,
the curve of a line,
the melody in a symphony of longing.
But I am the luckiest.
She is not just the muse of a fleeting work,
not merely a metaphor
etched into verse or rhyme.
She is the light that keeps the cold out,
the quiet gravity pulling all my chaos into place.
When I see her, the world softens,
like a puzzle finding its missing piece.
This is not about her perfection—
not about crafting her into an unattainable ideal.
It's about her being the heartbeat of my romance,
the pulse behind every word I write.
It's about me,
a flower blooming in the garden of her love,
petals reaching for her warmth,
roots grounded in the soil of her presence.
She is not the poetry itself—
she is the reason I believe
poetry exists at all.

Metaphors

Her face is fresh as a flower,
for time seems boundless,
when I look at her, every minute,
every hour. Is it she in her brilliance or is it the moon itself?
Her eyes are sheer poetry,
and her lips have the beauty of a lotus.
She is the thought of an artist,
and also, the meaning hidden in its translation.
She is some magical tale, the tale
in which pain and miseries are mere dust.
Her beauty is both dream and realisation,
for she is both certainty and supposition.
Her hairs are like no other, seen anywhere.
Splendidly luminous, dazzlingly radiant;
It is impossible to describe, that beautiful beloved.
To look at her is to become spellbound, and trust me,
this love that I have for her, this love, only in her, I found.
You remember when I wrote about you me the cookie and the coffee.
Well, that was one of the many metaphors I have in stock for you.
I have devoted my now
in writing my love for you.
For this now is all that I have to keep writing about you.
You're the chaos in my mind, and in your love, I sink.
You're the poem in my heart, and my love for you is the ink.

Aaditya Bajpai

Eyes

What do they say? your eyes?
With all that flame on the surface,
and hiding the softness inside.
They have hope, that you would try
to find glare amidst all the hazy hours.
Love, there's forever in your eyes.

Your eyes seek truth, because you
cannot fathom, living in the idea of void.
They are yearning to tell you, that you're
beautiful and you can reach so many heights.
Some angels are born with no feathers,
yet they are capable of making the highest of flights.

You called them boring and brown, but,
it were your eyes which I noticed first.
You envied the ones which others had;
love, only your eyes are filled with stardust.

How could you ever doubt yourself?
Those eyes you embody, so fearlessly bold.
Nobody could ever measure, not even the saints or
the poets; how much your eyes can unravel and hold.

Your eyes are the poem, the poem
of love, stars, and so much else in it.
They are selflessly beautiful, for
they hold on to things, they let things go.

This poem is what leads me to you,
for your eyes are the metaphor,
I have been yearning to write down.
I can no further define them, other than
to say that they are fearless and beautiful;
because to define is to put a stop to it,
to define is to limit.

Aaditya Bajpai

Butterflies

I hope you can tell me now,
am I the only one getting butterflies?
Or is it you too, who loses the world
when we are together,
looking into each other's eyes.
I cannot find the words to tell you,
how these calm feelings turn
into moments of anxious breathing
when you are not around.

I try so hard, not to make an
excuse just to call you every night.
There are born no words, to describe
how loved I feel when you're
around in my endure and every plight.
It's you and always you,
because without you, nothing,
not even my desperate self makes sense.

The world, the stars, the petals of a flower
nothing could ever match my love for you, immense.
How I would come to you with
my imperfections, my scars, my flaws!
And then you would show me
the stream of stars in my eyes,
a flame of fire in my breath and
the adventures entailed in my palm.
I see you in hefty crowds,
even in those empty fields
or the soaring clouds.

I hope you can tell me now,
am I the only one blushing around?
Or is it you too?
I want to dissolve in you,
to be so intensely close to you
that my own self disappears, because I see me in you.

Aaditya Bajpai

February

This familiarity between us, is evidence
that I have known you before.
How every smile, every whisper brings me
closer to the impossible conclusion that
I have known you before, I have loved you before
in another time, a different place, some other existence.

The flowers of February want you
to stay and shed your ivory light.
The joy you give and the spirit you entail,
your laughs and teases, and biting the nail.
It is a beautiful bliss, & all of it is true,
for loving you, is like winters with Bru.

Well now I am running out of excuses,
to stop myself from loving you.
This is chapter two of twelve,
for this is February, and this month is about you.
My winter ends with you, for you bring the spring.
And loving you is like eating oranges in February,
or drinking hot chocolate, or some cranberry.

If You Were by My Side

Stay still, let the moment pass,
let this restless heart settle—
but how do I stop you?
How do I quiet the storm of you
that rises every time I think of your face?

My sorrows would slip away,
fade like shadows at dawn,
if only you let me fill my eyes with you,
if only we spoke in the silence of glances,
if only you were by my side.
If you were by my side.

Flowing as one,
like a lake merging with a river,
your world becomes my world.
I would mould myself
into your every shape,
bend to your every current,
if you were by my side.

But your eyes hold a dream
heavy with disappointment and despair.
You carry the belief
that the heart's language
is nothing but deceitful whispers,
false echoes in the wind.

And so,
if you are by my side or not—
does it matter?
Life, cruel as it was before,
remains unyielding,
even with your shadow next to mine.
Even if you were by my side.

Aaditya Bajpai

Forever

The sky blooming with stars
and I was staring at you.
The chuckle on your face
and the glitter in your eyes,
I am so in love with you.
I urge the night not to turn day,
and I wish for you to rest your head
on my shoulders and stay.
You are the collection of all the
love letters that I have written.
For each and every text of it
yearns for you.

Why is it always so difficult
to even make an eye contact,
or to talk to you out there?
All I want is for you to just
stay, breathe and look in my eyes.
Because that, that is the most
beautiful feeling in the world.
You make everything make sense.
Without you, I am just half the man
I am supposed to be. Hence,
there's nowhere else that I'd be
without you.
For love is just a word,
without you.

Aaditya Bajpai

I Found You

I met you, at a point
when I needed you.
I had no manifestation, of you
or of the feeling that I have for you.
I never expected to fall
so early and miserably.
But with you, it was all
so simple and comfortable.
Even the darkest of nights
seemed enlightening enough.
In you I found the feeling,
of love and I found in you, hope.
I wasn't planning on falling for anyone,
but then you came into my life.
And that, that was it, for
you became a part of me.
I found you, I found myself;
I found myself wanting to spend
more time with you.
I found myself writing
my now for you.
I had nothing to hold on to,
but then I met you.
It was then when I realised
I have something worth fighting for,
that I have something worth holding on to.
This poem is what leads me to you,
for you are the metaphor I have been
yearning to write down.
You're half of me now, and
and my life is the fairy tale
of which you are the crown.

Unambiguous Ivory

Sitting right beside you
I would appreciate your hair.
That smile which you would give
even fairer than the word, fair.

I must warn you if you ever read this,
that it can make butterflies sound like
sun kissed hummingbirds.
I would pray from heart
If you could ever be mine
through all of my desperate words.

Being cynical is everything
that my eyes are about.
But being beautiful is just a part
of everything that you are about.
The melody to my lyrics,
or the syaahi to my poems.
You are all the references that
poetic literature is about.

Grace and beauty walks with you,
even the cupid falls on earth to have a sight!
The moon bows down to you,
and begs for some ivory light.
Your gaze has seared my heart so bad,
I hope it's not in vain.
I want to drown in your eyes forever,
never to surface again.

In your glimmering eyes I see, the magic of a moonlit night.
Your breath is what exists around me,
carrying my heart away like a weightless kite.
I am a hopeless romantic,
but this all isn't random.
For Your love, is the most unambiguous one
that these cynical eyes could ever fathom.

Aaditya Bajpai

Red

You see how I am always
looking into your eyes, with
a flicker of hope in mine, that
everything would turn around;
for us to be together, show us ways.
It's always for you; with you, and
never could I ever imagine a, without you.
My life is in you, and you
are the source of life in me.
You're the core to my flower,
which always stays, unlike the
petals which leave as the day fades.
I'll always love how you would melt
when I put my arms around you.
These poems aren't capable enough
to tell the world exactly how I felt.
You're the love that I feel, and
you're the feeling that I love.
You're the light, lighting my flames,
and you're the Red, in my veins.
You're the poetry in my heart,
in hope and in times of distress;
and you're the **_syaahi_** to my art,
and the answer to all my requests.

This isn't everything that I feel for you,
or the first time that I have written for you.
But this _now_ is all that I have,
to keep writing about you.
Be it the sun dying in the ocean,
or the moon coming up to take its place;
be it the stars being jealous of your beauty,
or be it the sunlight piercing through the haze;
everything about me is about you,
and with you, all my answers are true.

Aaditya Bajpai

Afraid

I'm afraid I'll lose you to someone
who can make you your favourite coffee,
and keep you out of your miseries,
better than I could ever do.
I'm afraid I'll lose you to his blossoming love,
which shall be glittered with
all the wondrous virtues of the world,
which I could never give.
I'm afraid I'll lose you to my times of endure,
that my darkness shall push you away.
I'm afraid I'll lose you to
someone else's mornings, or evenings
where he shall make love to you
as if it's an art.
I'm afraid I'll lose you
to another broken heart.

Wintertide

Wintertide means the times when winter subsits. We all want the winters to affect us in the ways we desire, be it in an unsympathetic way for some, or in a comfortable forgetting way for others. Winters don't last forever. I want the winters to not last eternally, for I am waiting for my sunshine to arrive, bringing the warmth of her soul and I just want to sleep in her lap. (Spring).

I don't want the winters to go away yet. For I still want to write about you, keep writing about you, every dusk and dawn, with a cup of tea in my hand, coffee sometimes. Winters make me make up stories about you and about how I did not fall in love with you, rather I fell in love with the idea of believing you. These stories give me words to write poetry about you and if winters are gone, where would my words come from. Like water, land and light is essential for the survival of humankind, Poetry is needed for the existence of Love, hope and magic.

You find poetry in winters and poetry comes to you in winters. Poetry is everywhere. Your hand is the ink, your eyes are the words, your lips are pen, and your heart is the paper. Believe me at last, you are the Poem.

What about the world? The world stays in its limits in winters to not disturb me while writing poems for you, about you. This "Now" is all that I have to keep writing about you, for even if we are not there, the memories of us will still exist in these poems.

But everything's up to these winters. I am hopeful still. I'll keep writing these winters down, and make the yellow of my diary, blue.

Till then,
Adieu.

Wintertide Poet's Vision (Pen Lips & Paper Heart)

The reason behind equalling Pen to lips and Paper to heart is that, heart is very fragile like a piece of paper, and the lips from where we make the words come out are very sharp. Like the way, in a normal course of life, the paper looks good as long as we are writing on it with the pen gently. The moment gentleness fades away, the paper starts deteriorating. Similarly our heart is also very fragile like a paper, and if we don't get or write words on it through our lips gently then it will get broken. That's the essence of poetry. You will get your ideas from their eyes, and you will find words from their lips and eventually she will be engraved as a poetry in your heart, which is the paper here.

December Again

December stands still, yet moves within itself,
a solemn breath before the year exhales.
The air whispers secrets of frost and fire,
a quiet warmth nestled in the heart of cold.

Beneath bare trees, life lingers,
fragile as the glass ornaments we cradle,
shining and trembling,
aware of their fragility.

It is the month of hands—
hands to hold close,
hands to wave goodbye.
Snow falls like memory,
each flake a piece of what was,
melting as it lands.

The sky wears both dawn and dusk together,
an endless twilight
where time folds in on itself.
The past feels closer,
the future a breath you cannot catch.

Love in December is fierce,
burning against the chill,
because it knows it must.
Because it knows
it will soon have to let go.

And so, we wrap the year in ribbons,
in the ache of holding on,
in the grace of release.
December, you are the stillness of endings,
the weight of beginnings,
a lesson in everything
we can never quite keep.

Aaditya Bajpai

Have I Gone Gray?

I Often wonder what it would be like if the world had no colors?

Without blue to mark the sky, how would I even know where the ground ends or begins? The sky wouldn't care; it never does. It's me—*I* need the blue, the reassurance. But without color, would I even need reassurance? It would all be the same. A shapeless, blank thing, indifferent to whether I saw it or not.

No. If there were no colors, would I still feel anything? Would love still have a place in this strange, hollow space? Colors bleed into everything—maybe feelings are just the shades I wear inside. A soft red for love, a cold blue for sadness. If they disappeared, what would that leave me with? Could I still feel love without the red? Would I even know if she was next to me?

Maybe I wouldn't need to feel her anymore. Maybe warmth would exist without the red to dress it. Maybe it's all just a glow, like two moons caught in orbit. But even moons need light. Without the sun, they're nothing. Am I nothing? Am I just a reflection, existing only because of something else? Something that isn't there?

But... maybe that's not emptiness. Maybe it's the beginning of something else, something beyond the colors that have fooled me into believing they mattered. Perhaps the love remains, even when I can't see it.

What if color *is* love? What if red isn't just a hue, but the pulse in my chest? If I lose that red, what happens to love? Would I even be able to touch her in a colourless world? Can touch exist without the proof of color? Without the feel of warmth against skin?

Maybe I wouldn't need hands anymore. Maybe I wouldn't need to touch. I could just exist, like a thought floating in endless gray, sensing without seeing. Knowing without proof. A love that doesn't ask for evidence. But... can love survive without proof? Wouldn't it all fade, blur into the same endless shade, like a flat line on a blank canvas?

Hasn't it already?

Aaditya Bajpai

Maybe life itself is just nothing layered on nothing, a story told through colors I never even chose. If I stripped it all away, what would remain? Would I recognize what's beneath? Or maybe I've already seen it—and I've forgotten. Maybe that's why I keep coming back to this same thought, the same question. What if there are no colors? What if there never were?

I think I've already had this conversation with myself. Over and over. Like an echo trapped inside my mind, circling back to the same point.

A thousand times, and yet, here I am. Still searching for color in a world that might have never had any. Or maybe... the world never lost its color. Maybe it's just me. Maybe I'm the one who's gone gray. And I don't even realize it.

Oranges & You

She peels an orange, separates it in perfect halves,
And gives one of them to me.
If I could wear it like a friendship bracelet, I would.
Instead I swallow it section by section, and tell
Myself it means even more this way.

You can find the tiniest bits of romanticism in places or objects or beings, that you might have never thought of before. Yes, Romanticism exists, for as humans, Love is the thing we do the best.

For you I want to share this cosy evening in a wintered Tokyo, and peel oranges, sharing a half with you and then you asking for the other as well for you want the warmth. I love you for life and still can't say that for I know I'll lose you, but here I am wanting to spend more time with you, wanting to peel one more orange with you.

The greatest lovers in the history of Romanticism have had the opportunity to love in ways they wanted to but did what they had to for they never wanted the love to fail, and I love you.

"... peeling oranges this ... sharing tangerines that ... what about cutting and de-seeding pomegranates for the ones you love? the ruby stains on your fingers ... fleeting proofs of your undying devotion ..."

Yes, peeling an orange with you today, and every day is everything this lover of yours has ever hoped or wished, wishes for because you are the most beautiful piece of poetry that I have ever read. You're the juice to my orange and I shall write poems for you no matter how much time it takes for you to love me.

All hopeless romantics are idealists, sentimental dreamers, imaginative and fanciful when you get to know them. They often live with rose coloured glasses on. They make love look like an art form with all the romantic things they do for their special someone.

For her. So I speak in a language she doesn't know.
"Je t'aime. Aujourd'hui. Ce soir: Demain. Pour toujours. Si

Aaditya Bajpai

je vivais mille ans, je t'apparti-endrais pour tous. Si je vivais mille vies, je te ferais mienne dans chacune d'elles"

I love you. Today. Tonight. Tomorrow. Forever. If I were to live a thousand years, I would belong to you for all of them. If I were to live a thousand lives, I would want to make you mine in each one.

I don't want to "have" a "conversation" I want to peel an orange and share it with you.

I love you.

Aaditya Bajpai

Amber

looking at your hairs
coming on your face
in this beautiful September.
i keep falling for you
for you are beautiful
and your eyes, **amber**.

like autumn leaves,
soft whispers flow,
each glance of yours,
a gentle glow.

the wind may dance
and trees may sway,
but my heart is still
when you pass my way.

your laughter lingers,
a melody sweet,
in this golden season
where our souls meet.

with every breath,
this truth feels new:
September blooms
because of you.

Nothing

My love for you still whispers,
soft as the wind through the leaves,
carrying the weight of words unsaid,
hoping that someday,
somehow,
it shall be heard.

But now,
when the echoes fade
and silence settles where you once stood,
I understand—
grief is the price we pay for love,
a debt of the heart,
etched in every tear
and every lingering memory of you.

Yearn

The stars faded away,
retreating into the void,
as though they couldn't bear
to witness my longing.

Even the wind mourned that night,
its whispers carrying
the ache of your absence.

The elements of the universe cried,
their grief entwined with mine,
when you slipped out of my sight.

Seeing me yearn for you,
even the moon, steady and silent,
bled softly in my plight,
its light dimmed by the weight
of a love left behind.

Polaroid

With the moon sneaking up
from the ocean at night,
its light spills over the waves,
and I remember you.

That Polaroid photo of ours,
still hanging on the wall of my bedroom—
a frozen fragment of time
where love felt infinite.

In it, I am kissing you by the beach,
the salt of the sea forgotten,
your warmth the only thing I knew.
I found solace in you then,
as though the world could break
and I would still be whole.

Now, the moon rises alone,
and the Polaroid fades softly,
but I keep it,
because it still carries the weight of you.

Aaditya Bajpai

Expresso

She is like a shot of expresso,
so rageful at times, yet
so, caring likewise.
She is like the recital
of that poem which stays.

She is like a cup of hot chocolate
so sweet from the first sip itself.
She is like the recital
of that poem which stays.

How at the coffee shop,
I would sit still, staring at you,
while you explode your heart out,
and i just wanna say, I love you.

She is like the bright sunshine
in days of despair and grief.
She is my knight in shining armour,
my saviour at the darkest of hours.

She is like the lyrics of that song
which will always be appreciated.
She is the one I had fallen for, and
ever since my heart's been alleviated.

How at the coffee shop,
I would sit still, staring at you,
while you explode your heart out,
and i just wanna say, I love you.

Be it the sunrise or the when sun sets,
or be it even in those dreary rains;
I think of you every,
now and then.

How at the coffee shop,
I would sit still, staring at you,

Aaditya Bajpai

while you explode your heart out,
and i just wanna say, I love you.

Aaditya Bajpai

Bookstore

I held the book you once read,
its pages still breathing your touch,
its spine bending under the weight
of a memory I can't let go.
February 12 lingers like a soft echo,
a date etched into the quiet spaces of me.

You sipped your coffee,
its steam mingling with the light,
while I sat silently crafting poems in my head,
each word born of your presence.
My tea blossomed in the wind of love,
its warmth no match for the fire
you kindled in me.

When we stepped out of the café,
the world shifted—
every step you took felt sacred.
As we wandered towards the bookstore,
I would have worshipped the ground you walked on,
if only to keep your path eternal,
if only to keep you near.

Aaditya Bajpai

Till Death do us Apart

Shivering, much isn't it ?
Manifesting thyself, in you.
Like a leaf falling, in Autumn,
knowing, will die, yet falling.
This all never ends,
the manifestation, of you.
Every page of my book,
bleeds, you.
For it shall never be dead,
in my head, it shall stay.
The love, that I felt, I feel,
I have it, still.
That scar I left, though upon you
stretches towards me.
Within the soul, it still exists,
you, your eyes and what we felt.
I left a void, my fault, my pain.
I say it out now,
my heart, still beats, in your soul.
I live in a fairy tale, knowing,
I might not yet deserve you.
Yet, I tell you how,
your name exists, in each and every
drop of blood that stays within me.
You're not here, still
you, me and the heart
till death do us apart.

The Girl I Met

It was then, when I met, this girl.
Brown hairs, and sheen in her eyes.
Just a glimpse of her,
that lightened up my skies.

The next day, I went to the same place,
with showers of sunlight upon my head,
I saw her, reading a book,
waiting, a little far away, just to get a look.

We were connected,
I knew that, somewhere and somehow.
All that was needed, was a flicker,
a flicker of light.

It happened, we talked.
From favourite flowers,
to zodiac signs,
all of it was beautiful, and
I was about to say it all.

It was since then, that I don't remember,
her name, the place, the world, anything.
It's all blank now, back to the darkness,
back to somewhere, that I don't know.

All that was left in my head,
was a blurred portrait of hers.
I tried looking around, asking people,
but the darkness had just grasped me so tight.

This all bothers me,
strikes my conscience,
creates a hole in it and
it hurts.

I think it was some,
faded memories, distant past, or some dream.

Aaditya Bajpai

At the darkest of the Hours,
amidst the ocean of stars,
while falling asleep.

Aaditya Bajpai

Seek

Through the stars
the light sends fair speechless messages.
The words of which,
are the manifestation of what I feel.

As the color grows darker,
all I pray for is to make this an everlasting night.
Or to stop the time at that particular moment,
when you smile.

Nothing seemed right,
until it was for you.
To this broken lamp,
like a source of light
came you.

I seek not, blessing.
Nor the flowers of cupid
to fall from above.
I seek hope and light,
The light, in you
I find.

Aaditya Bajpai

Touch

It isn't going anywhere,
the world, the blues.
It won't stop shining,
the stars, the moon.

Dwelling deep
into the waves,
and getting high
digging my own grave.

If only you could
touch my soul,
and lift me up.
My world would be
enlightened again.

For You

Though,
I, might not be true.
Still, all I wish for
is you.

Though,
I stumble upon
every problem, out there.
Still, all I wish is,
for you to pick me up.

Though,
I enjoy this
immense darkness in me.
Still, all I wish is,
for you to bring light.

Though,
I am no superhero.
Though,
I cannot promise you stars.
Though,
I cannot promise you hope.
Still, all I believe is,
you are my light,
you are my blues.

Though,
It might take time.
But, until the end,
all that I wish for,
is you.

These Letters

Nothing seemed right,
until it was for you.
To this broken lamp,
like a source of light
came you.

These letters won't bother you,
for they won't ever leave my place.
The ink would just get dry,
and who knows, one day
these letters might get lost in haze.

Just the moon will know,
what all you meant for me.
Just the stars will know,
all the letters that I wrote to you.

These letters,
though so many,
yet they all depict the same.
I won't ever stop writing them,
for these are my escape.
You are not close enough,
still I am close to you.
Because,
Nothing seemed right,
until it was
for you.

Aaditya Bajpai

Falling For You

In darkness,
your eyes give light.

Thoughts and Thinking,
happen all night.

In the itching sun,
your shadow gives relief.

In weakness,
your portrait instils belief.

In death
I felt more alive.
And it was all
because of you.

I am gonna
say it all loud.
That,
I can't help
falling in love with you.

Aaditya Bajpai

Mystery

The light of the day,
didn't seem bright enough.

The dimness of the dawn
didn't make me care enough.

The voice at the shore,
didn't make me blissed enough.

The beauty of the moon,
didn't seem alluring enough.

But then my eyes turned,
towards you.
Never had I ever seen such,
such mystery.
All I wanted was to,
to get lost,
into the mystery
and then I never wanted,
for it to get solved.

Aaditya Bajpai

My World

It never seemed right
until it was for you.
To this forgotten candle,
like a light, came you.

Darkness, my old friend,
stabbed me in the back.
To heal this wound,
like a cure, came you.

In death you were the one
who made me feel most alive,
and it was then when I knew,
why the world doesn't seem good,
I have been looking at the wrong place,
because my world, that's you.

I Met Her

I met her,
when the day was drowning,
birds, wandering,
and the sun was about to kiss the blues.

A stranger in
an unknown town.
I met her,
when I was down.

It's been some years,
since I met her.
Obviously we talked,
shared pain, amidst
the tumult of town.

Never saw her again,
maybe she went along
with life.
because I did too.

Aaditya Bajpai

White Rose

They all do the same,
meet, talk and fall.
But life's too short,
to go with the flow.
The thrill in making,
a story, is fascinating.
What's the worth,
if what you did
was done by every single hair.
Be the one,
who does the unseen.
Love like a white Rose,
rarely seen.

Aaditya Bajpai

Release

Into the shadows,
I am lost.
For you to love me,
I tried, at all costs.

It is all cold, now
which was once warm.
Everywhere,
there are storms.

My soul,
it calls for release.
Not in parts,
but all at once.

I know,
there won't be ease.

Under the Weight of Winter

The blanket is not just fabric,
it's a geography we might share,
a map of warmth sprawling between us,
where corners fold like unanswered questions.

Coffee—
it isn't just a drink tonight.
It's molten amber,
a quiet rebellion against the frost,
steam rising like breath
we didn't know we were holding.

You,
an unwritten chapter,
settling into the margins of my solitude,
your presence heavier than the snow
pressing against the windowpane.

The evening—
it doesn't belong to the world outside.
It bends to us,
its edges blurred by the hum of silence,
as if winter itself is pausing to listen
to the way we don't speak,
but still understand.

I want to share this with you,
not because the cold demands it,
but because the weight of your absence
is heavier than any blanket.

Aaditya Bajpai

The Burn

The coffee is scalding,
but I don't notice,
because the fire isn't in the cup—
it's in your gaze,
in the way your hands curl around porcelain,
as if cradling the world.

I sip too soon,
the heat bites,
but it's nothing compared to the way
your laughter spills like sunlight,
sharp and soft all at once,
cutting through the fog of this moment.

My lips sting,
but all I can see is the curve of yours,
the way they press to the rim
like a whispered secret.

The burn stays,
a quiet reminder that even pain
feels like warmth
when it's born in your presence.

Aaditya Bajpai

The Walk

Let's walk,
your hand in mine—
not as an anchor,
but as a quiet tether
to this fleeting moment.

You talk,
words spilling like rivers,
each one carving soft canyons
into the air between us.
I barely hear them,
not because they don't matter,
but because you do.

I watch the way your lips shape each syllable,
the way your eyes light with every thought,
and it feels like the whole world
is moving in step with us.

The ground blurs beneath my feet;
I can't recall the path,
only the cadence of your voice
and the rhythm of your heartbeat
as I hold your hand,
pretending the world outside
doesn't exist.

A Sunflower for You

I want to give you a sunflower,
not because it's beautiful,
but because it turns its face to the light,
just as I turn to you.

Its petals—
golden, imperfect, radiant—
are the kind of quiet brightness
that reminds me of the way
you fill a room without trying.

I imagine placing it in your hands,
watching the way your fingers curl around its stem,
delicate, but certain,
like you've always known
how to hold something alive.

The sunflower isn't a gift;
it's a mirror.
It carries everything I cannot say:
how you are the sun
and I am just trying to bloom in your orbit.

Aaditya Bajpai

Beyond Mountains

I want to live with you
in the world beyond mountains,
where the sky folds itself into silence
and the air tastes like beginnings.

There, the sun spills its gold carelessly,
and we gather it,
threading its light into the fabric of days
that belong to no one but us.

The mountains are not boundaries—
they are the edges of a map
we'll draw together,
fingers tracing valleys and peaks
like secrets we've yet to discover.

No roads will lead to us,
only whispers of wind
carrying our names in languages
we'll never speak aloud.

I want to live with you there,
where time forgets itself
and every shadow is softened
by the weight of your presence.

Aaditya Bajpai

The Sweater: Offering

I want to share my sweater with you,
not because it's cold,
but because it's the only way
to let you linger on me.

I'd drape it over your shoulders,
watch it swallow you whole,
the fabric carrying your shape
as if learning the weight of love.

Later, I'd wear it myself,
pulling it close,
not for warmth,
but for the faint memory of your scent,
woven into every thread,
clinging like a whisper.

It's not the sweater I want to wear—
it's you,
stitched into the quiet spaces of my day,
a presence soft and unshakable,
so that even when you're not here,
you are.

The Sweater: Woven Memory

And when I wear it again,
it's no longer just mine.
It carries your laughter,
your touch,
the way your fingers brushed the hem
like a fleeting thought you didn't speak.

The sleeves stretch differently now,
holding the memory of your arms,
as if the sweater itself
has learned what it means to hold you.

Each thread hums with your absence,
but not in sorrow—
it hums because you were here,
and here is everywhere you've been.

I want to share my sweater with you,
because it isn't just a sweater anymore—
it's us,
stitched into something that will never unravel.

Aaditya Bajpai

The Sweater: Threads of Us

And when the days grow colder,
I'll pull it tighter,
as if holding onto the pieces of you
that still fit into the seams.

It will remind me of our quiet moments,
of how you'd smile when the world felt too loud,
and I'd watch you,
knowing that the warmth was never in the fabric,
but in the space between us.

Even if the sweater frays over time,
its threads unravelling at the edges,
it will still hold the shape of you,
softened by wear,
but unbroken,
just like the way I carry you with me—
in every crease,
in every stretch.

And so, I will wear it,
not as a garment,
but as a promise—
that even in the silence,
we are always wrapped together.

Aaditya Bajpai

The Sweater: Fading Warmth

And when the sweater fades,
its color dulled by the seasons,
I'll remember how it once held us,
how it once captured the warmth of your presence,
woven into the fabric of every moment.

But the threads, worn and thin,
will never be the same—
they will be you,
and me,
intertwined in ways we can't undo,
even as time pulls at the edges.

If it tears, I won't mend it,
because some things are too perfect in their imperfection.
I'll let it be—
a memory hanging from my shoulders,
as fragile as love,
but as enduring as the space
we made together in it.

In the end,
the sweater will be a testament
not to what was,
but to what remains—
a piece of you,
a piece of me,
woven forever into the fabric of now.

The Sweater: Evermore

And when the sweater finally unravels,
I'll let it go,
like I've let so many things slip through my fingers.
But the threads will still be here—
in the way I remember your smile,
in the quiet moments when I swear I feel you near.

It will not be the end,
for we will always have the warmth
we once wore,
woven in the quiet places between us.

The fabric will return to dust,
but in the dust, there is no loss.
There is only a quiet knowing
that we shared something unspoken,
something that will never leave me,
even when there is no sweater to hold.

And I'll carry that warmth forever—
not in the fibres,
but in the part of me
that always belonged to you.

Aaditya Bajpai

The Last Letter

Maybe you will never read this.
Maybe these words will slip through time,
falling into the cracks where memories lie—
hidden, waiting to be unearthed
by fingers that won't know the weight
of the paper or the echo of my voice.

But if you do,
if you find these letters after the days
have lost their meaning,
after the stars have forgotten how to shine
in the space between us,
know that they are not just ink and paper,
they are the breath of the silence
we couldn't speak aloud.

Perhaps you'll understand
that in the way the world spins
without ever asking if we're still here,
these words will stay.
They will remain in the air,
like forgotten songs sung to an empty room.
They will grow like vines,
twisting through time,
catching on the edges of things
that have long since faded.

I have written to you,
not because I believe you'll read them,
but because there is something eternal
in the way love leaves traces—
in the way you never really go,
no matter how far the years stretch.

These letters will be the ghosts of us,
silent and waiting in corners
where the world can't touch them.
They'll be immortal,
not because I wanted them to be,

Aaditya Bajpai

but because I never could let go of you—
not even after everything ends.

Aaditya Bajpai

I wrote you endless letters, each one a piece of me, yet they lie unread. Do I keep them close to feel your absence, or burn them to feel your warmth, even if just for a moment?

Perspective

The romanticism of orange flowers can be characterized by the confluence of a multiplicity of evocative features. This chromatic and olfactory combination is imbued with a subtlety and richness that is unparalleled in its ability to evoke a sense of longing and desire.

The hue of orange is inherently linked to warmth, vitality, and dynamism. It is a hue that is undeniably uplifting, evocative of the sun and the fertile earth. The allure of orange flowers is further enhanced by their delicate, intricate structures. The petals are intricately arranged in a symmetrical and harmonious fashion, creating an organic geometry that is both mesmerizing and seductive. When viewed from a distance, the flowers appear as a vibrant orange blur, an ethereal presence that seems to glow with an inner radiance.

However, if one looks at this picture closely then the beauty of the orange flowers might be overlooked by the human race for their eyes shall be focussed on the barren lands behind. The juxtaposition of the orange flowers amidst the dry, barren lands creates a striking visual dichotomy. The vibrant hue of the blossoms seems almost surreal

Aaditya Bajpai

against the dull and lifeless landscape. It is as if nature itself is making a bold statement, asserting its resilience and determination to survive. The flowers' delicate petals sway in the unrelenting heat, a reminder of the fragility of life, yet also of its tenacity. It is a scene of contrasts, of beauty amidst decay, of hope amidst despair. The orange flowers serve as a beacon of light in the darkness, a small but powerful symbol of nature's ability to endure and flourish against all odds.

In the presence of the orange flowers amidst the barren land, human tendencies are often marked by a desire to assign purpose to their existence. Questions arise, such as "what is the point of these flowers in such a desolate landscape?" This inclination towards rationalization can obscure the inherent beauty of the scene and reduce it to mere functionality. It is as if we seek to impose our own sense of order onto the natural world, to explain away the inexplicable. Yet the orange flowers defy such narrow-minded thinking, existing simply because they can, a testament to the whims of nature and the beauty that arises from its unfettered expression. In a world increasingly defined by human intervention and control, the orange flowers serve as a reminder of the intrinsic value of the natural world and the importance of embracing the beauty that arises from its inherent chaos.

The orange flowers' mere presence in a barren landscape subverts the human impulse to impose order and rationality, instead offering a glimpse into the unpredictable, yet exquisite, manifestations of the natural world. It is a display of nature's raw, unbridled power, a force that has no need for human rationalization or purpose. Rather, it is an entity that is self-sufficient, infinitely complex, and wholly deserving of appreciation in its own right.

"Amidst the barren lands, some orange in flowers blooms,

personifying a flicker of hope in the desolate gloom.

The vibrant hue, acting as a beacon of life

in the midst of an arid terrain, existing as a

testament to nature's resilience, despite the parched pain.

Each petal, a brushstroke of colour on a canvas of dust and sand, a masterpiece of contrast, the perfect blend of desolation and grand.

For even in the bleakest of landscapes, life finds a way,

to bloom and thrive, to shine and stay."

The End

"If You Do Find Her" – **A Note To Readers**

As you reach the final words of this book, I want to leave you with something unspoken, something that lingers beyond the pages. These letters were never just for me to write; they were for you to read, to feel, and perhaps even to understand. They were written in moments of silence, in the spaces where words don't quite reach. They exist in a place where time and distance no longer matter, where love is neither defined nor understood fully—but always felt.

If, in some strange turn of fate, you happen to find her—the one these letters were meant for, whether she walks beside you in the present, exists in the quiet of your past, or resides in some distant corner of your heart—show her these words. Let her know that this is what was left unsaid, this is what was always meant to be felt but never quite spoken.

Perhaps, in reading these letters, she'll understand something that was always hidden in plain sight. Perhaps she'll recognize herself in the spaces between the lines, in the pauses, in the longing that never truly disappeared. But if, for whatever reason, you do not find her, let these letters remain as they are—fragments of a story, pieces of a puzzle that were never meant to be completed. They will exist as whispers, always waiting, always unfinished.

So, if you do find her, in whatever form, wherever she may be, take these letters and let them tell her that she has always been here. That her absence was never empty; it was simply the canvas for something larger. Show her that she was written into this, and that in the end, it was always about waiting for her to understand—if she ever does.

The Artist's Touch

Aadi Jain

This is to appreciate the incredible talent of **Aadi Jain**, my brother, who crafted the stunning cover design for *Letters to Her*. His ability to translate emotions and stories into visuals is truly remarkable, making every detail of the cover a reflection of the depth within the book. Aadi's creativity and artistic vision shines through in this piece, showcasing his exceptional skill.

I highly encourage everyone to explore more of his work by visiting his Instagram handle **@aartsie_**. If you're looking for something unique and beautifully designed, don't hesitate to approach him.

Challenge: Write A Poem To Your "Her" Here